Columbus

Cooperative Game-in-a-Book

by Mary Pearce

No part of this publication may be reproduced in whole or in part, or stored in a retrieval system, or transmitted in any form or by any means, electronic, mechanical, photocopying, recording, or otherwise, without permission of the publisher. For information regarding publishing, write to Scholastic Professional Books, 730 Broadway, New York, NY 10003.

Cover design by Vincent Ceci Cover and interior illustration by Laszlo Kubinyi Design by Patricia Isaza

12 11 10 9 8 7 6 5 4 3 2

ISBN 0-590-49206-3
Copyright 1992 © by Scholastic Inc.
Printed in the U.S.A.

1 2 3 4 5/9

Welcome to *Columbus Cooperative Game-in-a-Book!*

On the pages that follow, you'll discover a host of exciting—and cooperative—ways for your students to explore Columbus's historic voyage to the New World in 1492.

CONTENTS	
List of Materials	this page
Set-Up Instructions	this page
Playing Instructions	3
Gameboard Extension Activities	4
Spinner; Ship Playing Pieces	5
Crew Cards	7
Cargo Cards	11
Travel Cards	13
New World Cards	17
Gameboard	bound in center
Columbus Cooperative Mini-Unit	21
Bibliography	24

THE NEW WORLD ENCOUNTER GAME

In this fun, fact-based game, your students simulate Columbus's rich—and rugged—journey from Palos, Spain, to San Salvador in the New World, and back again. To make the game ready to play, follow the quick and easy **Set-Up Instructions** on this page. The step-by-step **Playing Instructions** are on page 3.

GAMEBOARD EXTENSION ACTIVITIES

On page 4, you'll find inventive strategies for using the gameboard poster to teach geography, directional skills, Columbus facts, and much more.

COLUMBUS COOPERATIVE MINI-UNIT

On pages 21-23, you'll find lots of fresh, classroom-tested ideas for teaching Columbus across the curriculum. Included are activities designed for language arts, social studies, math, and science.

BIBLIOGRAPHY

And, finally, on page 24, you'll find an extensive bibliography. To round out your Columbus Unit, here's a list of the very best books and educational materials available.

Columbus Cooperative Game-in-a-Book has the potential to enrich your classroom teaching in so many ways. Now it's time to turn the pages and explore.

THE NEW WORLD ENCOUNTER GAME

Materials:
- 4 Ship Playing Pieces
- Spinner
- **Brass Fastener** (not included)
- **Paperclip** (not included)
- 24 Crew Cards: 4 Captains, 4 Senior Officers, 4 Idlers, 4 Petty Officers, 4 Able Seamen, 4 Ship's Boys
- 12 Cargo Cards: 4 Drink, 4 Crew's Food, 4 Officers' Food
- 32 Travel Cards
- 16 New World Cards
- Gameboard

Set-Up Instructions:
1. Open this book to its center and carefully remove the staples.
2. Unfold the gameboard and place it on a table.
3. Cut out all the Crew, Cargo, Travel, and New World Cards. Place them in separate piles.
4. Cut out the ship playing pieces and spinner. Follow the easy instructions for constructing both on page 5.

THE NEW WORLD ENCOUNTER GAME

PLAYING INSTRUCTIONS

Object:
Players reenact Columbus's historic journey by moving their ships from Palos, Spain, to San Salvador in the Bahamas, and back again.
The player who has collected the most points upon returning to Palos is the winner.

Number of Players: 2-4

Directions:

1. Each player begins the game with a ship placed on Palos, Spain, and 9 cards as follows:
- **A Full Crew:** 1 Captain, 1 Senior Officer, 1 Idler, 1 Petty Officer, 1 Able Seaman, and 1 Ship's Boy.
- **A Full Cargo:** 1 Drink, 1 Crew's Food, and 1 Officers' Food.

Players take turns reading aloud each of the Crew and Cargo Cards. They should place their cards on the designated spots on the gameboard.

2. Shuffle both the Travel Cards and the New World Cards. Place them on the correct spaces on the gameboard.

3. Spin to see who goes first. The player spinning the highest number goes first; the other players take their turns in order, going clockwise from player 1. Players must move their playing pieces the designated number of spaces each time they spin the spinner (unless the spinner lands on *Take a Travel Card*).

4. Players may move up, down, or across in any direction. A player may not move diagonally.

5. If a player lands on the following special spaces by *exact count*, he or she should do the following:
- **Danger Space:** Lose a turn.
- **Suerte Space** (SWEAR-tay means *luck* in Spanish): Move 7 spaces in any direction.
- **Travel Space:** Take a Travel Card from the top of the pile, read it aloud, and follow its directions. A player directed to lose a Crew Card or Cargo Card, places it on the Sea Monster. A player directed to gain a Crew Card or Cargo Card, takes it from the Sea Monster. If the designated card is not on the Sea Monster, a player collects nothing. Travel Cards are returned to the bottom of the Travel Card pile.

6. A player must land on San Salvador by *exact count*. Then he or she spins again and collects New World Cards as follows:
- Spin a 1: 1 New World Card
- Spin a 2: 2 New World Cards
- Spin a 3: 3 New World Cards
- Spin a 4: 4 New World Cards

(If they spin *Take a Travel Card*: they *don't* take a Travel Card, but *do* spin again until they get a number.)

7. A player must land on the space for Palos, Spain, by *exact count* to complete the game. The following points are awarded to the finishers in this order:
- 1st: 4 points
- 2nd: 3 points
- 3rd: 2 points
- 4th: 1 point

8. Players calculate their scores by adding their finish points to their Crew, Cargo, and New World Card points. The winner is the player who has collected the highest number of points.

Game Variation:
For a shorter version of the New World Encounter Game, end the game when the first player has landed back on Palos, Spain, and been awarded 4 points. The 2nd, 3rd, and 4th place finishers are calculated by who is the second, third, and fourth closest to Palos (*closest = fewest number of spaces away from Palos*). Players add their finish points to their Crew, Cargo, and New World Card points. The player with the most points wins.

Game-in-a-Book: **COLUMBUS**

GAMEBOARD EXTENSION ACTIVITIES

To enrich The New World Encounter Game, share some of these gameboard extension activities with your students before or after playing.

Tracing Columbus's Route

On the gameboard, locate Columbus's original route to San Salvador in the New World, and then back to Palos, Spain. (Both are labeled.) Share these routes with students. Then use the Scale of Nautical Miles (located at the bottom of the gameboard) to calculate *approximately* how many miles Columbus traveled from Palos to San Salvador (3,950 miles), and back to Palos (4,100 miles).

We know that it took Columbus about 41 days to sail from Palos to San Salvador (that's not counting the 29 days he spent in the Canary Islands). With students, calculate *approximately* how many miles he averaged per day. Per hour?

Understanding Directions: North, East, South, and West

Point out the compass rose (located at the bottom right of the gameboard). Discuss how a compass rose works; how it shows the directions of north, east, south, west, northeast, southwest, etc. Reinforce directional skills by asking students questions such as: In which direction was Columbus traveling on his way to the New World? (southwest, then west) In which direction was Columbus traveling on his way back to Spain? (northeast, then east)

Remind students that Columbus's plan was to sail west to Asia (which he never did reach). On a world map or globe, show students where Asia is located. Then ask questions such as: Did Columbus take the shortest route to Asia? In which direction(s) should he have sailed to take the shortest route to Asia?

Learning the Names of Places: Then and Now

Share with students this fact: When Columbus landed on *Guanahani* he renamed it *San Salvador*. Then read the names of the other cities, islands, and countries on the gameboard: Palos, Spain; San Salvador; Hispaniola; etc. Help students to locate those same places on a current world map. Ask questions such as: Have any of the names changed over the years? Why do you think some of the names have changed? Do you think Columbus had the right to rename the islands he encountered in the New World?

Using the Columbus's Journey Timeline

Read the timeline out loud. (It's located around the perimeter of the gameboard.) Then ask students what they think is the single most important event highlighted: Departing Palos? Landing on San Salvador? Feeling hopeless? Returning home at the end of the long journey? Encourage students to support their claims. If you like supplement the timeline with more information from one of the many books listed in the Columbus Bibliography (see page 24).

Point out that on September 9th Columbus and his crew completely lost sight of land until reaching San Salvador on October 12th—over a month later! Discuss with students how Columbus and his men might have felt during their long, landless voyage: Restless? Scared? Lonely? Excited?

Comparing Europe and the New World

Share with your students the European "Old World" city scene (located in the lower-right hand corner) and the the North American "New World" scene (in the upper-left hand corner). Tell students that these are an artist's interpretation of what the two places looked like in Columbus's time. Ask students to compare the two: How are they alike? How are they different?

Supplement the discussion with other information students might have about these two "different worlds." Then follow-up the conversation with questions such as: How do you think it felt to go from one world to the other? Are these two places as different today? Why or why not?

4 Game-in-a-Book: **COLUMBUS**

How to make the Spinner:

Cut out spinner and poke a brass fastener through the dot in the middle. Open a paperclip into an S shape. Slide the narrow end of the S under the fastener. Then fold the ends of the fastener under the spinner. To spin, flick the wide end of the paperclip with your thumb and forefinger.

How to make the Ship Playing Pieces:

Cut out the four ships along the dotted lines.

To construct each ship:
Fold in half from right to left.

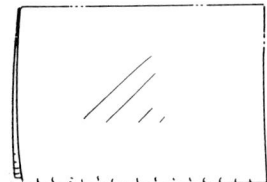

Fold down right corner.

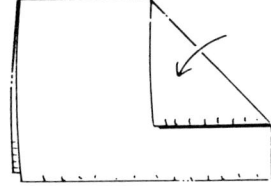

Fold down left corner.

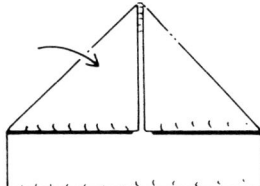

Fold bottom flaps up and ship will stand up. Color each ship a different color.

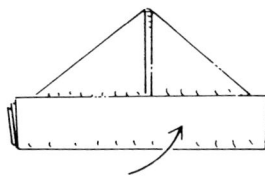

SPINNER

SHIP PLAYING PIECES

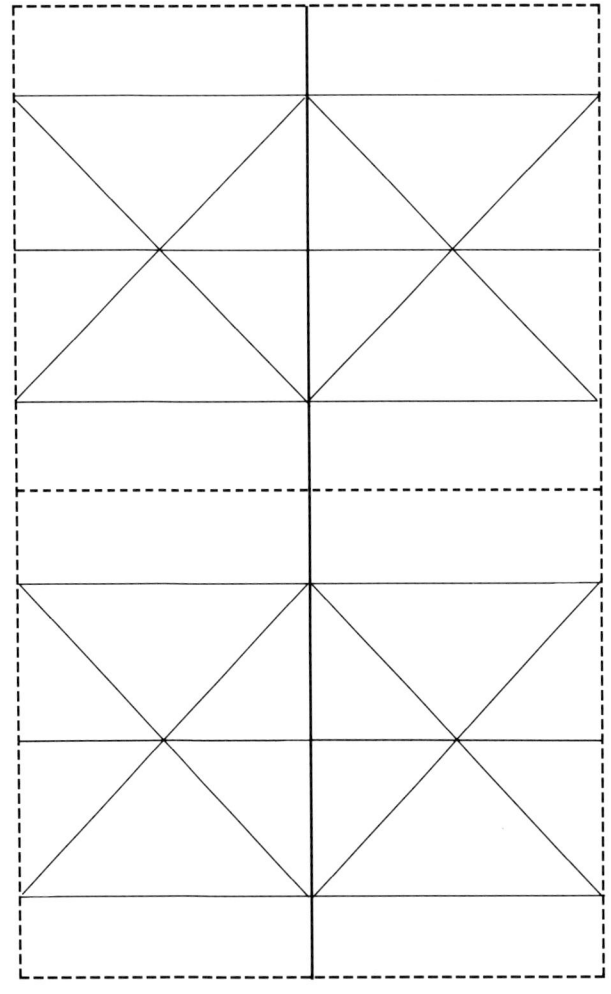

Game-in-a-Book: **COLUMBUS 5**

CREW CARDS

CAPTAIN — 6 POINTS	**SENIOR OFFICERS — 5 POINTS**	**IDLERS — 4 POINTS**
Columbus was the leader of the fleet and the captain of the *Santa Maria*, the largest ship. Martin Alonzo Pinzon was the captain of the *Pinta*, and his brother Vincente Yanez Pinzon was the captain of the *Nina*; both men reported to Columbus.	Columbus would have been sunk without his senior officers. Each ship had a *master*, who was second in command, and a *pilot*, who was the chief navigator.	The expedition also included "idlers," which was what sailors called people who did no physical work. The *secretary* was supposed to take notes on the voyage. The *interpreter* knew Hebrew and Arabic. And the *royal comptroller* kept track of the king and queen's gold.
CAPTAIN — 6 POINTS	**SENIOR OFFICERS — 5 POINTS**	**IDLERS — 4 POINTS**
Columbus was the leader of the fleet and the captain of the *Santa Maria*, the largest ship. Martin Alonzo Pinzon was the captain of the *Pinta*, and his brother Vincente Yanez Pinzon was the captain of the *Nina*; both men reported to Columbus.	Columbus would have been sunk without his senior officers. Each ship had a *master*, who was second in command, and a *pilot*, who was the chief navigator.	The expedition also included "idlers," which was what sailors called people who did no physical work. The *secretary* was supposed to take notes on the voyage. The *interpreter* knew Hebrew and Arabic. And the *royal comptroller* kept track of the king and queen's gold.
CAPTAIN — 6 POINTS	**SENIOR OFFICERS — 5 POINTS**	**IDLERS — 4 POINTS**
Columbus was the leader of the fleet and the captain of the *Santa Maria*, the largest ship. Martin Alonzo Pinzon was the captain of the *Pinta*, and his brother Vincente Yanez Pinzon was the captain of the *Nina*; both men reported to Columbus.	Columbus would have been sunk without his senior officers. Each ship had a *master*, who was second in command, and a *pilot*, who was the chief navigator.	The expedition also included "idlers," which was what sailors called people who did no physical work. The *secretary* was supposed to take notes on the voyage. The *interpreter* knew Hebrew and Arabic. And the *royal comptroller* kept track of the king and queen's gold.
CAPTAIN — 6 POINTS	**SENIOR OFFICERS — 5 POINTS**	**IDLERS — 4 POINTS**
Columbus was the leader of the fleet and the captain of the *Santa Maria*, the largest ship. Martin Alonzo Pinzon was the captain of the *Pinta*, and his brother Vincente Yanez Pinzon was the captain of the *Nina*; both men reported to Columbus.	Columbus would have been sunk without his senior officers. Each ship had a *master*, who was second in command, and a *pilot*, who was the chief navigator.	The expedition also included "idlers," which was what sailors called people who did no physical work. The *secretary* was supposed to take notes on the voyage. The *interpreter* knew Hebrew and Arabic. And the *royal comptroller* kept track of the king and queen's gold.

Game-in-a-Book: **COLUMBUS**

CREW CARDS

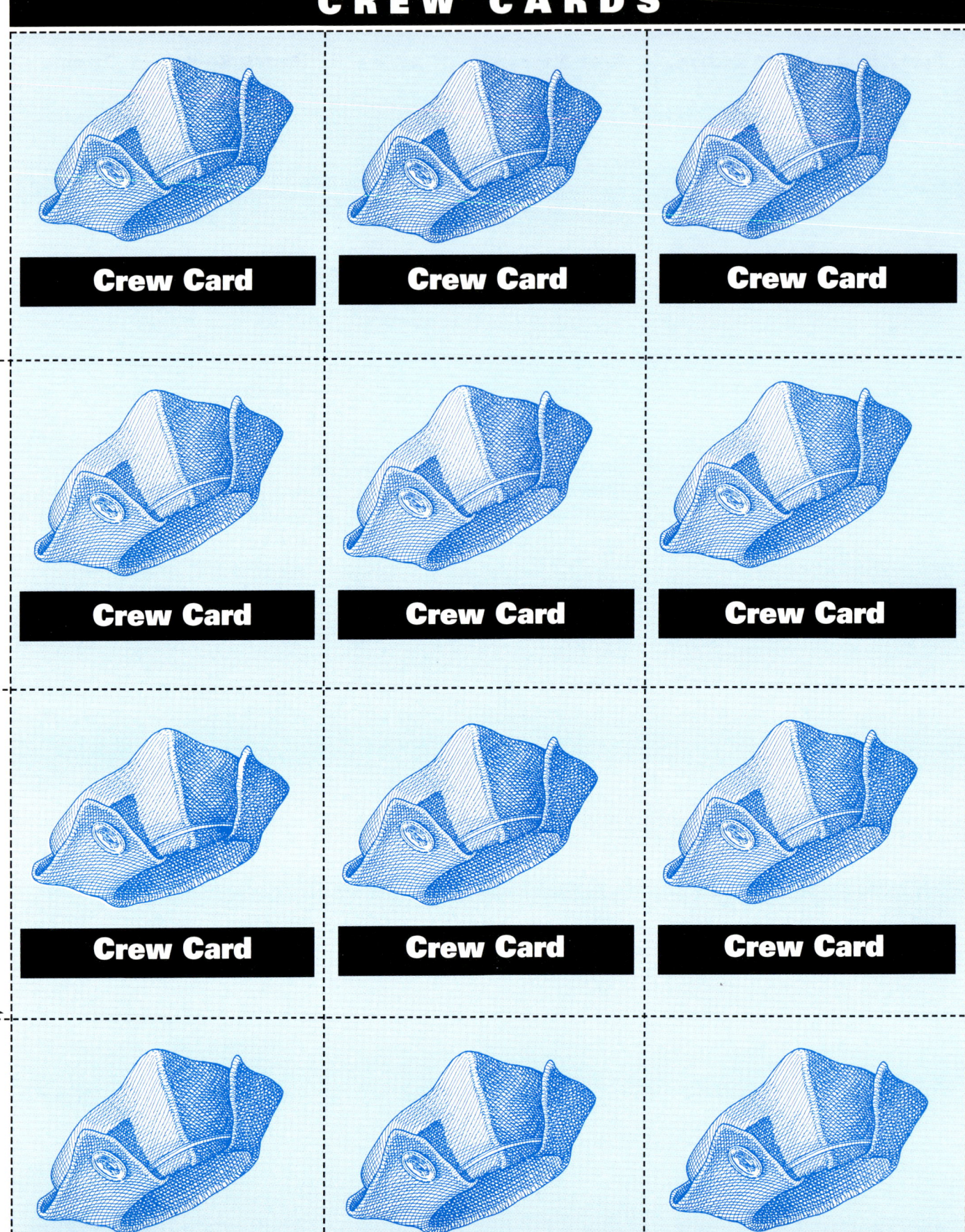

8 Game-in-a-Book: **COLUMBUS**

CREW CARDS

Petty Officers — 3 points

Each ship had four lower ranking officers. The *boatswain* was in charge of all the equipment. The *steward* kept track of food and supplies. The ship's doctor was called the *surgeon*. To break up fights, the *marshal* was on-board.

Able Seamen — 2 points

They were the ones who sailed the ships. Many were also skilled laborers. The *carpenter*, for example, had to keep the ships from falling apart. The *caulker* and the *painter* were always searching for those pesky leaks. And the *cooper* repaired the barrels, which contained the ships' supplies.

Ship's Boys — 1 point

These teenagers were on-board to learn to sail. They ended up doing all the chores no one else wanted to do: cooking the meals, turning the sandglass, and cleaning up after the captain and the rest of the crew. Most of them worked up the ranks to become able seamen.

Petty Officers — 3 points

Each ship had four lower ranking officers. The *boatswain* was in charge of all the equipment. The *steward* kept track of food and supplies. The ship's doctor was called the *surgeon*. To break up fights, the *marshal* was on-board.

Able Seamen — 2 points

They were the ones who sailed the ships. Many were also skilled laborers. The *carpenter*, for example, had to keep the ships from falling apart. The *caulker* and the *painter* were always searching for those pesky leaks. And the *cooper* repaired the barrels, which contained the ships' supplies.

Ship's Boys — 1 point

These teenagers were on-board to learn to sail. They ended up doing all the chores no one else wanted to do: cooking the meals, turning the sandglass, and cleaning up after the captain and the rest of the crew. Most of them worked up the ranks to become able seamen.

Petty Officers — 3 points

Each ship had four lower ranking officers. The *boatswain* was in charge of all the equipment. The *steward* kept track of food and supplies. The ship's doctor was called the *surgeon*. To break up fights, the *marshal* was on-board.

Able Seamen — 2 points

They were the ones who sailed the ships. Many were also skilled laborers. The *carpenter*, for example, had to keep the ships from falling apart. The *caulker* and the *painter* were always searching for those pesky leaks. And the *cooper* repaired the barrels, which contained the ships' supplies.

Ship's Boys — 1 point

These teenagers were on-board to learn to sail. They ended up doing all the chores no one else wanted to do: cooking the meals, turning the sandglass, and cleaning up after the captain and the rest of the crew. Most of them worked up the ranks to become able seamen.

Petty Officers — 3 points

Each ship had four lower ranking officers. The *boatswain* was in charge of all the equipment. The *steward* kept track of food and supplies. The ship's doctor was called the *surgeon*. To break up fights, the *marshal* was on-board.

Able Seamen — 2 points

They were the ones who sailed the ships. Many were also skilled laborers. The *carpenter*, for example, had to keep the ships from falling apart. The *caulker* and the *painter* were always searching for those pesky leaks. And the *cooper* repaired the barrels, which contained the ships' supplies.

Ship's Boys — 1 point

These teenagers were on-board to learn to sail. They ended up doing all the chores no one else wanted to do: cooking the meals, turning the sandglass, and cleaning up after the captain and the rest of the crew. Most of them worked up the ranks to become able seamen.

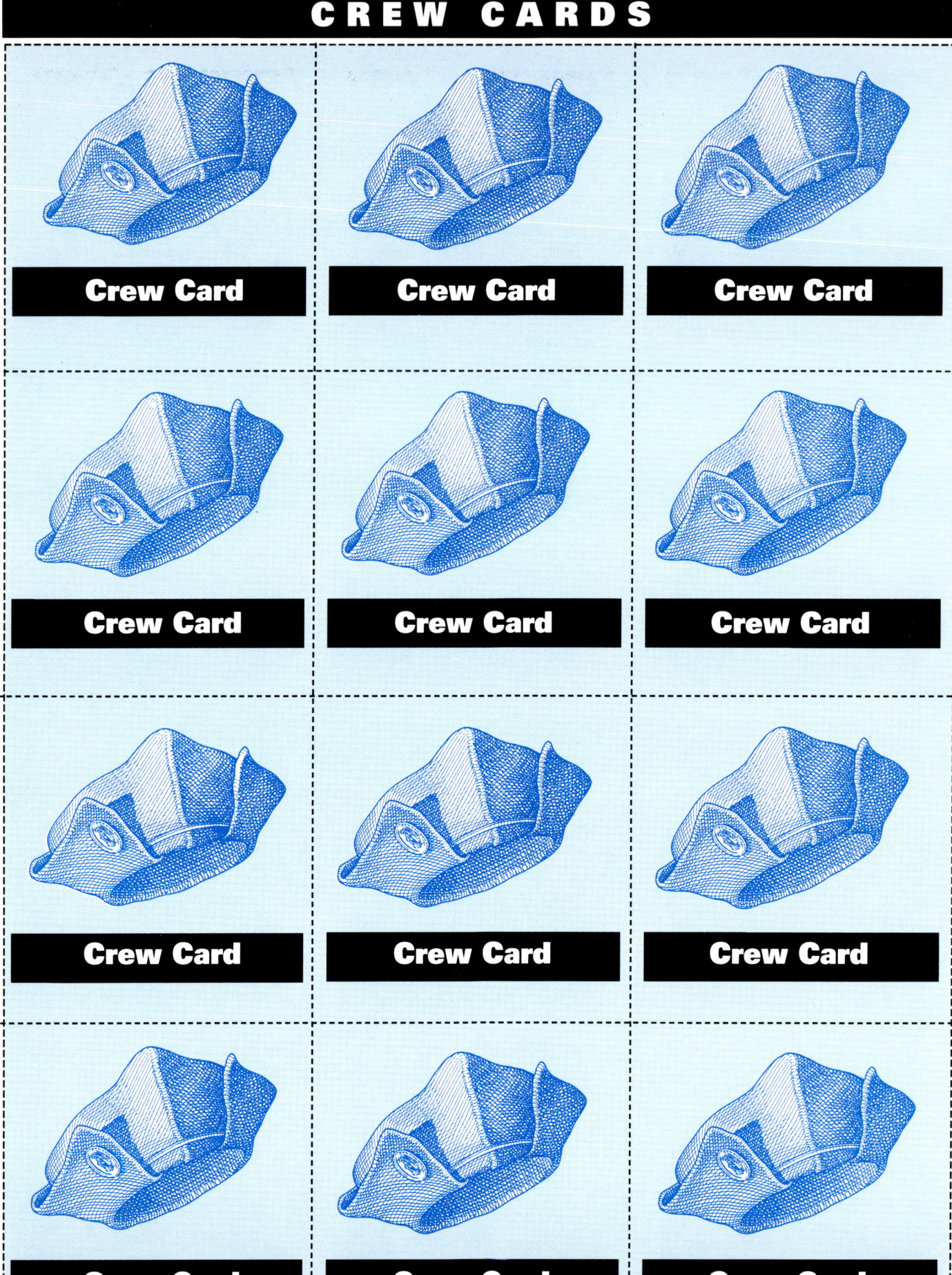

CARGO CARDS

DRINK 3 POINTS	**CREW'S FOOD** 2 POINTS	**OFFICERS' FOOD** 1 POINTS
Sailors drank both water and wine with their meals. Wine was preferred because it didn't go bad as quickly. Water was also used in making bread on-board.	The sailors really had no idea how big the ocean was. So they took along a year's supply of food. All three meals included salted meat and fish, hard biscuits, and dried chickpeas and lentils. Fresh fruits were eaten early in the voyage, before they rotted.	In addition to the crew's standard fare, officers might have cheese, almonds, and raisins. Some officers kept their own stashes of dried fruits, too.
DRINK 3 POINTS	**CREW'S FOOD** 2 POINTS	**OFFICERS' FOOD** 1 POINTS
Sailors drank both water and wine with their meals. Wine was preferred because it didn't go bad as quickly. Water was also used in making bread on-board.	The sailors really had no idea how big the ocean was. So they took along a year's supply of food. All three meals included salted meat and fish, hard biscuits, and dried chickpeas and lentils. Fresh fruits were eaten early in the voyage, before they rotted.	In addition to the crew's standard fare, officers might have cheese, almonds, and raisins. Some officers kept their own stashes of dried fruits, too.
DRINK 3 POINTS	**CREW'S FOOD** 2 POINTS	**OFFICERS' FOOD** 1 POINTS
Sailors drank both water and wine with their meals. Wine was preferred because it didn't go bad as quickly. Water was also used in making bread on-board.	The sailors really had no idea how big the ocean was. So they took along a year's supply of food. All three meals included salted meat and fish, hard biscuits, and dried chickpeas and lentils. Fresh fruits were eaten early in the voyage, before they rotted.	In addition to the crew's standard fare, officers might have cheese, almonds, and raisins. Some officers kept their own stashes of dried fruits, too.
DRINK 3 POINTS	**CREW'S FOOD** 2 POINTS	**OFFICERS' FOOD** 1 POINTS
Sailors drank both water and wine with their meals. Wine was preferred because it didn't go bad as quickly. Water was also used in making bread on-board.	The sailors really had no idea how big the ocean was. So they took along a year's supply of food. All three meals included salted meat and fish, hard biscuits, and dried chickpeas and lentils. Fresh fruits were eaten early in the voyage, before they rotted.	In addition to the crew's standard fare, officers might have cheese, almonds, and raisins. Some officers kept their own stashes of dried fruits, too.

CARGO CARDS

Cargo Card

Cargo Card

Cargo Card

Cargo Card

Cargo Card

Cargo Card

Cargo Card

Cargo Card

Cargo Card

Cargo Card

Cargo Card

Cargo Card

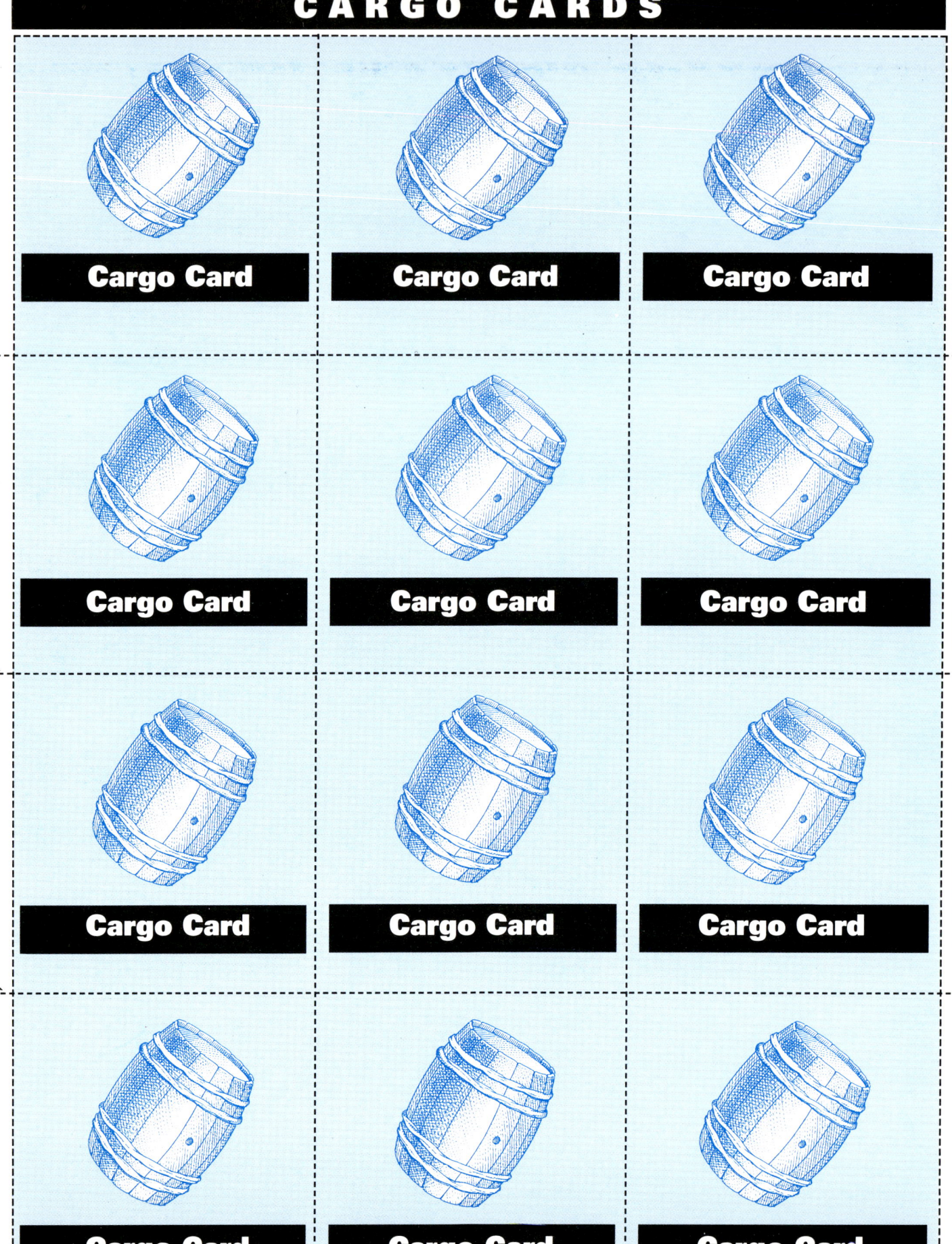

TRAVEL CARDS

It's a calm day. You have a chance to take a bath in the ocean. Your shipmates are happy you're smelling better. Move 2 spaces in any direction.	Someone is already sleeping in your favorite spot below deck. So you end up in a corner with a rat's nest and get little sleep. Lose your lowest ranking Crew Card to the Sea Monster.	You see a meteorite fall into the ocean. Some of the crew think it's a bad sign. Lose your lowest ranking Crew Card to the Sea Monster.
A ship's boy forgets to turn the sandglass when it runs out. You lose track of a few minutes, and the ship's boy goes to the brig. Lose your lowest ranking Crew Card to the Sea Monster.	The ship has taken on water during the night. So the pilot tells you to "work that pump brake till she sucks [the water out]." Lose your lowest ranking Crew Card to the Sea Monster.	You sail into an enormous patch of seaweed. The seaweed slows down the ships. Lose your highest ranking Crew Card to the Sea Monster.
The cooper tells a funny story, and the crew has a good laugh. Move west 2 spaces.	You get sores in the corners of your mouth—the first sign of scurvy. You trade your knife for a bunch of raisins that will keep scurvy away. Take any Cargo Card from the Sea Monster.	You haven't seen land in a month and are feeling very homesick. Move south 1 space.
A ship's boy sings, "On deck, on deck in good time, you of the pilot's watch. Shake a leg!" It's time for you to stand watch for 4 hours. Take the lowest ranking Crew Card from the Sea Monster.	All hands are called to evening prayer: "God give us a good night and good sailing; may the ship make a good passage." This comforts the crew. Move 3 spaces in any direction.	You are afraid you will never see land again. Some crew members are threatening to throw Columbus overboard if he doesn't turn back. Lose your highest ranking Crew Card to the Sea Monster.

Game-in-a-Book: **COLUMBUS 13**

TRAVEL CARDS

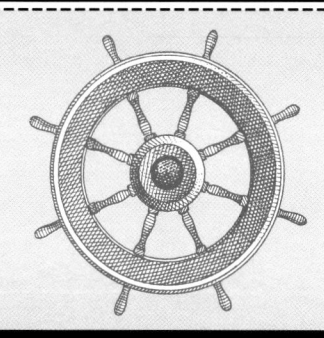 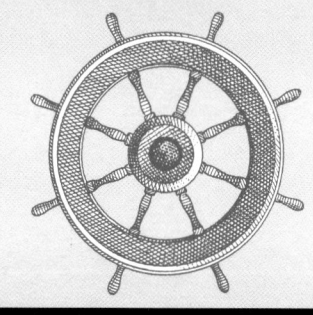 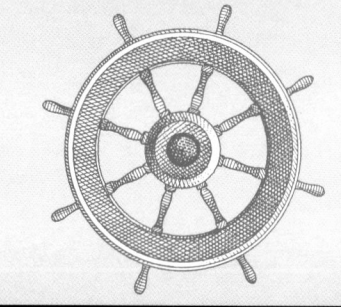

Travel Card **Travel Card** **Travel Card**

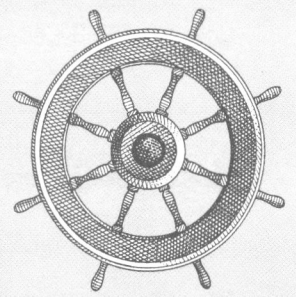 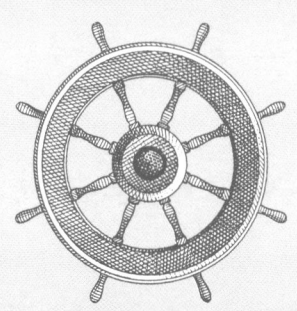 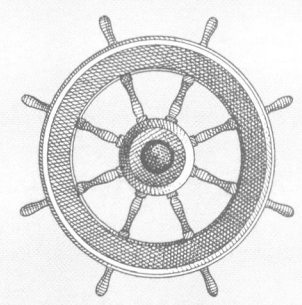

Travel Card **Travel Card** **Travel Card**

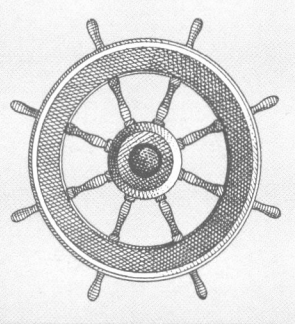 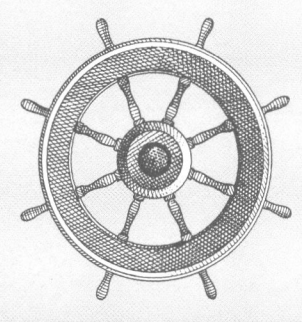 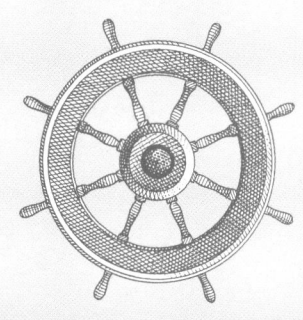

Travel Card **Travel Card** **Travel Card**

 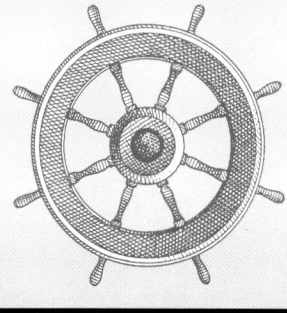 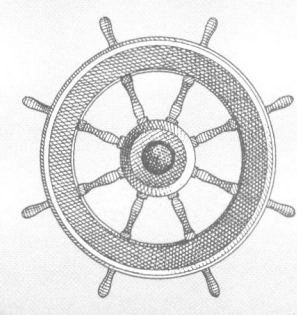

Travel Card **Travel Card** **Travel Card**

14 Game-in-a-Book: **COLUMBUS**

TRAVEL CARDS

You think you see land. But it turns out to be nothing but low clouds. Move east 1 space.	A flock of birds surrounds the ship. The crew is happy because it is a sign that land is near. Take the highest ranking Crew Card from the Sea Monster.	A ship's boy doesn't pay attention to the firebox on deck. The meat is so burned, you can't eat it. Lose any Cargo Card to the Sea Monster.
Many porpoises are surrounding the ship. You take this as a sign that land is near. Take the highest ranking Crew Card from the Sea Monster.	You bite into a biscuit and discover worms crawling through it. Next time you'll eat in the dark so you don't see them. Lose any Cargo Card to the Sea Monster.	You adopt one of the ship's 25 cats and name him *Suerte* (luck). You give him bits of your food, and he brings you all the rats he catches. Lose any Cargo Card to the Sea Monster.
The biscuit you were eating slipped from your hand and fell overboard. It sank like a stone. Lose any Cargo Card to the Sea Monster.	You spot a light in the distance, but only one other crew member saw it, too. You think your eyes are playing tricks on you. Lose your highest ranking Crew Card to the Sea Monster.	The men are grumbling about the long voyage. You tell them about the rewards they will receive at the end of the trip. They cheer up. Take the highest *and* lowest ranking Crew Cards from the Sea Monster.
You sailed 177 miles today. But you tell the crew that you have sailed only 132. This way they won't worry that they are too far from Spain to ever return. Move 2 spaces north, then 1 space west.	You need help with making and setting the sails and scrubbing the deck. Take the lowest ranking Crew Card from the Sea Monster.	A raging storm has pushed you off course. Move north 3 spaces, then east 2 spaces.

Game-in-a-Book: **COLUMBUS** **15**

TRAVEL CARDS

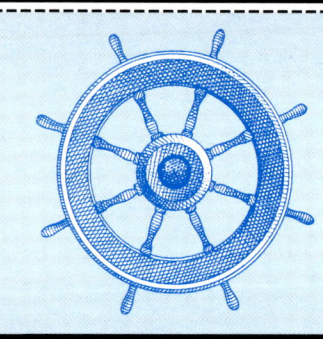
Travel Card

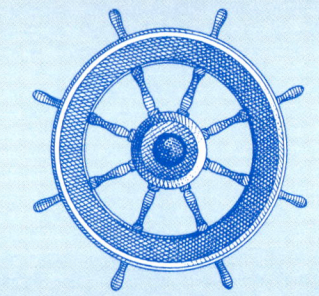
Travel Card

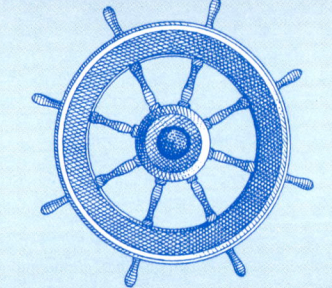
Travel Card

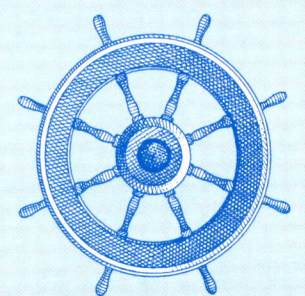
Travel Card

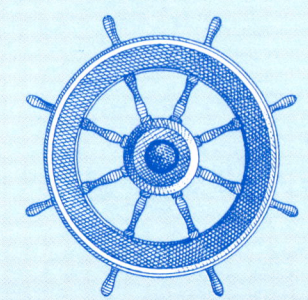
Travel Card

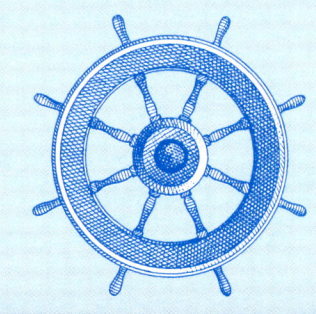
Travel Card

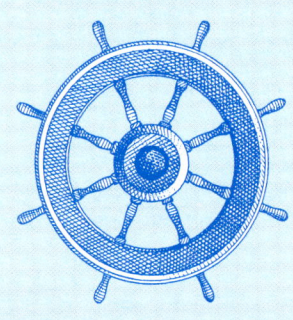
Travel Card

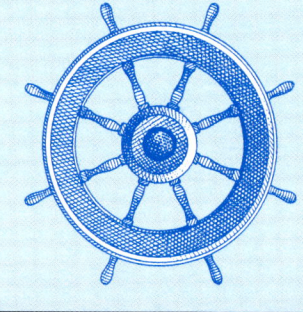
Travel Card

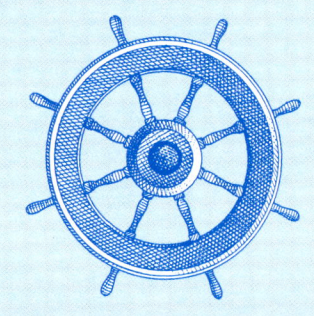
Travel Card

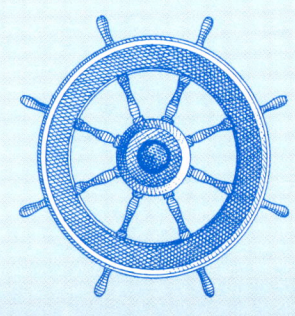
Travel Card

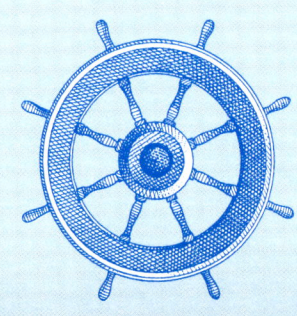
Travel Card

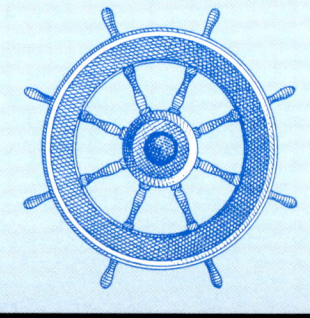
Travel Card

16 Game-in-a-Book: **COLUMBUS**

TRAVEL CARDS ♦ NEW WORLD CARDS

The high winds meant that all hands were on deck for two days. Now finally you can sleep. Move east 2 spaces.	You think about your friends and family in Palos. You start to wonder if you'll ever see them again. Lose your lowest ranking Crew Card to the Sea Monster.	**NEW WORLD CARD 1 POINT** Think of the Arawaks and other Native Americans when you eat popcorn, corn chips, and corn bread. They introduced corn to the Europeans.
Supplies are running low. The crew kills a porpoise and a very large shark for food. Take any Cargo Card from the Sea Monster.	You're afraid you won't make it back to Spain. So you write the King a letter about the voyage, seal it in a barrel, and throw it overboard. Lose your highest ranking Crew Card to the Sea Monster.	**NEW WORLD CARD 1 POINT** Think of the Arawaks and other Native Americans when you eat popcorn, corn chips, and corn bread. They introduced corn to the Europeans.
Your main mast is coming loose from the deck. Your crew tries, but still can't secure it. Move north 3 spaces.	An inexperienced ship's boy is steering the vessel. The officer who gave the boy permission to steer is in trouble. So is the ship's boy. Lose your highest *and* lowest ranking Crew Cards to the Sea Monster.	**NEW WORLD CARD 1 POINT** Think of the Arawaks and other Native Americans when you eat popcorn, corn chips, and corn bread. They introduced corn to the Europeans.
There has been lightning three times today, which is a sure sign a storm is coming. Move west 1 space.	The storm is so bad that you let your ship run before the wind. The wind carries you where it wants. Move south 1 space, then west 1 space.	**NEW WORLD CARD 1 POINT** Think of the Arawaks and other Native Americans when you eat popcorn, corn chips, and corn bread. They introduced corn to the Europeans.

Game-in-a-Book: **COLUMBUS**

18 Game-in-a-Book: **COLUMBUS**

NEW WORLD CARDS

NEW WORLD CARD 1 POINT You can thank the Arawaks and other Native Americans for tomatoes, which today are used to make spaghetti sauce, pizza, and ketchup.	**NEW WORLD CARD 1 POINT** Mashed, baked, or french fried, potatoes are one of our favorite foods. They were first grown in the New World.	**NEW WORLD CARD 1 POINT** Europeans first tasted cacao brewed as a bitter drink in the New World. They brought it back to Europe and added sugar to make the first chocolate.
NEW WORLD CARD 1 POINT You can thank the Arawaks and other Native Americans for tomatoes, which today are used to make spaghetti sauce, pizza, and ketchup.	**NEW WORLD CARD 1 POINT** Mashed, baked, or french fried, potatoes are one of our favorite foods. They were first grown in the New World.	**NEW WORLD CARD 1 POINT** Europeans first tasted cacao brewed as a bitter drink in the New World. They brought it back to Europe and added sugar to make the first chocolate.
NEW WORLD CARD 1 POINT You can thank the Arawaks and other Native Americans for tomatoes, which today are used to make spaghetti sauce, pizza, and ketchup.	**NEW WORLD CARD 1 POINT** Mashed, baked, or french fried, potatoes are one of our favorite foods. They were first grown in the New World.	**NEW WORLD CARD 1 POINT** Europeans first tasted cacao brewed as a bitter drink in the New World. They brought it back to Europe and added sugar to make the first chocolate.
NEW WORLD CARD 1 POINT You can thank the Arawaks and other Native Americans for tomatoes, which today are used to make spaghetti sauce, pizza, and ketchup.	**NEW WORLD CARD 1 POINT** Mashed, baked, or french fried, potatoes are one of our favorite foods. They were first grown in the New World.	**NEW WORLD CARD 1 POINT** Europeans first tasted cacao brewed as a bitter drink in the New World. They brought it back to Europe and added sugar to make the first chocolate.

Game-in-a-Book: **COLUMBUS**

NEW WORLD CARDS

New World Card	New World Card	New World Card
New World Card	New World Card	New World Card
New World Card	New World Card	New World Card
New World Card	New World Card	New World Card

20 Game-in-a-Book: **COLUMBUS**

Columbus
COOPERATIVE MINI-UNIT

LANGUAGE ARTS

A Question of Character

Who was Columbus and how has the popular perception of him changed with the times? Gather a variety of children's books on Columbus, one for every two students. Make sure you have books from 20 and 30 years ago, as well as books with recent copyrights. Divide the class into partners. Have each pair read a different book and discuss what Columbus was like. Consider such questions as:

- Was he an adventurer?
- Was he kind?
- Was he cruel?
- Was he a hero?

Ask a representative from each pair to report its findings to the class. Chart the findings. Then talk about the portraits presented in the books.

Speaking Without Words

When Columbus and his crew first met the natives of the New World, neither group knew how to speak the other's language. Ask students to pair off to discuss ways in which the Native Americans and the crew may have communicated with each other, such as hand and body language. Then have pairs volunteer to act out a meeting between a Native American and a sailor, based on the pair's earlier discussion. Suggest that the sailor try to make friends, communicate where the ships have landed, and convey the need for food and shelter. The Native American should give appropriate responses. Have students discuss the difficulty they had communicating without words and the ways they discovered to make their needs known.

Columbus-Inspired Logs

We know a lot about Columbus's voyages because he kept logs, detailed records of his journeys. Explain to students that a log is similar to a diary: it tells each day's routines, weather, and activities, the ship's location, and special events. Have students keep their own logs for a week. Then ask them to form small groups and read what they wrote to the other group members. Then have each group conduct a round robin discussion. Each group member in turn should tell the person to the right one thing he or she learned about him- or herself by keeping a log, such as specific likes and dislikes and favorite activities.

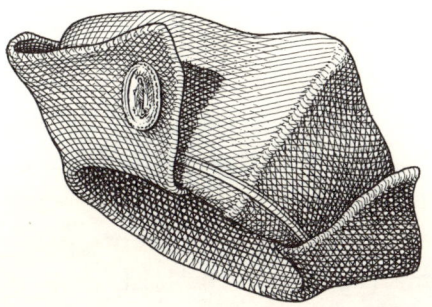

Game-in-a-Book: **COLUMBUS** 21

SOCIAL STUDIES

Journey Maps

When Columbus made his first trip to the New World, he drew maps that helped him find his way on later voyages. Have your students make maps of their routes to school by using the "Think, Write, Pair, and Share" strategy. Begin by having each child think about his or her route to school and then write simple directions, noting street signs and landmarks passed on the way. Then ask each child to find a partner who lives in the same neighborhood. The partners can share and refine the written directions and translate them into a graphic map. They can make their maps three-dimensional by using non-drying modeling clay, toothpicks, construction paper, and other materials to add street signs, buildings, and landmarks.

American Top-Ten Lists

When Columbus returned to Spain from the New World, he brought back Native Americans, as well as exotic animals and plants. These gave the Spanish an idea of what the New World was like. Have students pair off to discuss and agree upon a list of 10 items from our country that they might take to a faraway place to show its people what the U.S. is like. Ask each pair to explain why it chose the items on its list and what these things say about American life. For example, a hamburger from a fast food chain might indicate the eating habits of some Americans and suggest that Americans like quick, simple food they don't have to prepare themselves.

MATH

Creative Measurement

Today we still use many units of measurement that Columbus used. A yard, for example, was the distance from the king's finger to the tip of his nose. Brainstorm with students their own original units of measurement based on body parts. Then have each student turn to a partner, decide on one of these original units, and use it to measure distances in the classroom and school playground. For example, student pairs may measure how many "pinkie-fingers-long" their desks are and how many "giant-steps-long" the playground is. Ask each pair to report its measurements to the class, then discuss how these measurements compare with real measurements and why it is important that everyone uses the same measurement.

Cargo Calculations

On a sea voyage like Columbus's, the person in charge of supplies had to figure out how much drinking water to take along so that each person would have enough water to survive the journey. Divide students into small groups. Explain that a person should drink about eight 8-oz. glasses of water a day. Using this rule, have students in each group put their heads together to figure out the amount of water each of them would need on a sea voyage if it lasted two days, a week, a month, or a year. Then ask students to discuss what they might do if they lost their drinking water. Encourage them to come up with creative solutions to this problem.

Soda-Bottle Sandglasses

Exactly every half hour on board the *Santa Maria*, a ship's boy said a prayer. How did he know when a half hour was up? The sands of the *ampoletta*, or sandglass, had run out. Here's how students can make their own sandglasses. Each student or small group of students will need two identical clean one-liter soda bottles with caps, a nail, heavy-duty tape, two boxes of table salt, and a watch with a second hand. Students should follow these steps:

1. Remove both caps. Tape the top sides together. Use the nail to poke a hole straight through the tops of both caps.

2. Fill one bottle about three-quarters full of salt. Screw on the double cap.

3. Turn the empty bottle upside down and screw it to the double cap.

4. Turn over the bottles. Time how long it takes for all the salt to run from the top to the bottom.

SCIENCE

Compass Connections

Columbus used a compass to determine in what direction he was traveling. A compass needle will always point north. To demonstrate this, have pairs of students make compasses. Each pair will need a half-inch slice of bottle cork, a magnet, a sewing needle, a bowl of water, and the following directions:

1. Float the cork in a bowl of water.
2. Stroke the needle against the magnet five or six times in the same direction, rather than backward and forward.
3. Place the needle on the floating cork. The needle will turn so that one end will always point north.
4. After finding north, label the sides of the bowl north, south, east, and west.

Pulley Partners

Columbus's crew often used pulleys to lift supplies on and off his ships. Pulleys are still used for this purpose today. Have students pair off to make their own simple pulleys. Each pair will need an empty thread spool, two lengths of string, about 6 inches and 24 inches long, a pencil, and the following directions:

1. Thread the shorter string through the spool and tie the ends together.
2. Use this string to hang the spool on a doorknob or another convenient place.
3. Tie a pencil to one end of the longer string.
4. Put the other end of the string over the spool and pull down on this end to lift the pencil. Have each pair use the pulley to lift other objects, too. Ask each pair to come to an agreement about why pulleys make lifting easier and share its findings with the class. You may wish to provide more advanced students with a second pulley and more string. Challenge them to figure out how to attach the second pulley and decide what effect the second pulley has on how many objects can be lifted.

Charting Constellations

Columbus relied on the stars, as well as on a compass, for direction. As a clear-night homework assignment, have students use an encyclopedia and astronomy books to help them locate the Big and Little Dippers and other constellations in the sky. When they return to school, supply each student with a piece of black construction paper, a white crayon, and a pin or pencil. Ask each student to do the following:

1. Select a constellation.
2. Use the white crayon to mark the location of its stars on black construction paper.
3. Use pins or pencil points to make holes where the stars are marked.

Here's how to make a classroom planetarium:

1. Cut out one side of a closed box whose side is slightly smaller than the black construction paper.
2. Place a strong flashlight or filmstrip projector inside the box.
3. Cut long slits a half-inch from the open end.
4. Slide a student's pinhole constellation into the slits. In a darkened room, the pinhole constellation will be projected onto the wall or ceiling.

Game-in-a-Book: **COLUMBUS** 23

BIBLIOGRAPHY

Books (grades 2–3)

All Pigs on Deck by Laura Fischetto (Delacorte, 1991)

The Discovery of America by Betsy Maestro (Lothrop, Lee & Shepard, 1991)

Follow the Dream by Peter Sis (Knopf, 1991)

In 1492 by Jean Marzollo (Scholastic, 1991)

Books (grades 3–5)

Christopher Columbus: From Vision to Voyage by Joan Anderson (Dial, 1991)

Christopher Columbus: Voyager to the Unknown by Nancy Smiler Levinson (Dutton, 1990)

Columbus: For Gold, God, and Glory by John Dyson (Simon & Schuster, 1991)

I, Columbus: My Journal edited by Peter and Connie Roop (Walker, 1990)

I Sailed with Columbus by Miriam Schlien (HarperCollins, 1991)

If You Were There in 1492 by Pam Conrad (Caroline House, 1991)

The People Shall Continue by Simon Ortiz (Children's Press, 1987)

Westward with Columbus by John Dyson (Scholastic, 1991)

Where Do You Think You're Going, Christopher Columbus? by Jean Fritz (Putnam, 1981)

Who Really Discovered America? by Stephen Krensky (Scholastic, 1987)

Books (grades 5 and up)

Admiral of the Ocean Sea: A Life of Christopher Columbus by Samuel Eliot Morison (Oxford University Press, 1942)

Columbus and the World Around Him by Milton Meltzer (Franklin Watts, 1990)

The Conquest of Paradise by Kirkpatrick Sale (Knopf, 1990)

First Encounters: Spanish Explorations in the Caribbean and the United States, 1492-1570 edited by Jerald T. Milanich and Susan Milbrath (University of Florida Press, 1989)

The Log of Christopher Columbus translated by Robert H. Fuson (International Marine Publishing, 1991)

The Log of Christopher Columbus' First Voyage to America as copied by Bartholomew Las Casas (Linnet, 1989)

A People's History of the United States by Howard Zinn (Harper & Row, 1990)

The Southern Voyages: 1492-1616 by Samuel Eliot Morison (Oxford University Press, 1974)

Other

Columbus 500 Publications offers the following educational packets:

- **Christopher Columbus and His Voyage of Discovery,** a teacher's guide for grades K-3 that includes activities, background, a play, calendars, posters, a timeline, and activity patterns for $7.95

- **Christopher Columbus and His Encounter with the New World,** a teacher's guide for grades 4-7 that includes simulations, background, maps, timelines, task cards, ship patterns, and a play for $7.95

- **The Columbus Connection,** a 20-page student activity guide for grades K-7 that includes a gameboard, ship reproducible, science projects, a play, maps, and cut-outs for $3.95

To place an order, write Columbus 500 Publications, P.O. Box 1492, Medford, NJ 08055, or call (609) 953-3218.

24 GAME-IN-A-BOOK: **COLUMBUS**